Foreword

Out of the mouth of babes, as the old saying goes. *Prayers for Grandparents* is the essence of simplicity: it shows just what can emerge when young people are given freedom to express themselves.

This book comes at a very important time for all of us involved in the transmission of the faith. As the Catholic Grandparents Association have said on so many occasions, everyone can be someone who passes on the faith – you don't need to have an in-depth knowledge of scripture, all you need is a prayer or a hymn on your tongue, and a desire to imbue in others a love of God and of his message.

These prayers touch all the emotions. They are joyful and uplifting in places – 'They believe in me, they bring me to the seaside, and ask me over for tea.' They make you curious for more information, to know something else of the family life, and in the terseness of the language, they are deeply sorrowful and touching: 'Dear Granny and Grandad, why did you have to go? I hope you are in a better place with God by your side.'

Prayers for Grandparents emerges from a new impetus in the Catholic Church, an impetus that first took root in the west of Ireland, with the establishment in 2007 of the National Grandparents Pilgrimage. In just a few short years, the value of Grandparents in the Church has come to prominence. There is a sense that the time of grandparents has arrived; where families are broken and fragmented, it is often the grandparents who provide a crucial, unwavering sense of constancy to the children.

As Patron of the Catholic Grandparents Association, I commend to you *Prayers for Grandparents*. As one contributor, Chloe, writes in her prayer, grandparents 'are kind, helpful, careful and generous, and they look after Keelan and me very well'.

Dr Michael Neary,
Archbishop of Tuam

Dedication

We would like to dedicate this book to St Joachim and St Anne, Parents of Mary, Grandparents of Jesus; and to all grandparents, alive and deceased, for all they have done for us down through the ages, particularly in the transmission of the faith.

Acknowledgement

We would like to acknowledge and thank in particular the children of Ireland for writing such wonderful tributes to their grandparents. We wish to thank our patron Archbishop Michael Neary, and all who worked so hard to bring this little book to fruition: Caitriona in Veritas; Grace and Caroline at Knock Shrine Museum, who helped select the prayers; Noreen, who helps everyone with everything; and Maire Printer for her commitment and hard work. We feel sure that this little book will encourage greatly all grandparents in their marvellous vocation of passing on the faith and will bring blessings and graces to all who read it.

Catherine Wiley

Father in heaven,

please pray for my grandmother and
my grandad. He is in heaven so will you
please mind him, and will you tell him
that I always loved him. Tell him who I
am because I didn't see him, I was a
baby. I hope you will still pray for my
granny, and I will pray for you.
Amen.

The first prayer received by the CGA

Dear God,

thank you for my granny and
grandad. I'd like you to take
care of my granny in the hospital
because she is sick.

Chynell Carroll

6

Dear God, thank you for my grandparents. They believe in me, they bring me to the seaside, and ask me over for tea.

They teach me things I never knew. How I love my family, and you.

I never knew my grandad Doyle, but if he was here he would make me smile, so bless them, Lord, and for them I will pray, each and every single day.
Amen.

Stephanie Holligan

Grandparents

I just wanted to say thank you
for my grandparents that love me
and care for me and are always
kind to me. Even if they are not
young, they still have lots of fun!
Amen.

Conor Kennedy

8

A Better Place

Dear Granny and Grandad, why did you have to go? I miss you every day and every night. How much I love you.

I miss you all the time. My family also misses you, and my uncle too.

I hope you are in a better place with God by your side. Thank you God.

Amen.

I ♥ you

Granny and Grandad: you're kind and
protective, you're sweet and you're nice.
You care for my future and what I do with it.
You say I'm smart and if there's something I
want, I try and I'll get it. You just want the
best for me, and when I go to your house,
great stories you tell. The thing I'm trying to
say is ... 'I love you' Granny and Grandad!

Keep Them Safe

To God: bless my nana and granda. They are very special to me. Keep them safe, especially my granda in heaven — I really miss him. Please Lord, keep them safe. My nana and granda are the best thing ever; they buy me everything.

Shannon Joyce

Dear God, since I only have one grandparent, please make her safe because she means the world to me and I want her to live for years more. I still pray for my grandad that passed away last year – all my family miss him so much. He means the world to me as well and I love the memories of the times I had with him and I love the memories I have of my gran and I would hate to think that there is something going to happen to my gran. I hope my dog Minnie that passed away in January is with my grandad because they loved each other and they need company. Please make all my family and my animals safe.

Hannah

Healthy Life

Dear Jesus, please let my grandparents, Maureen and Brendan, live a long and healthy life. We make this prayer to thank the Lord.
Amen.

Thomas Cannon

Grandad

Granny

God bless my grandparents – they're kind and gentle. They're not like other people who are completely mental. They would always offer you something to eat; if there was a fire on they would say, 'Put up your feet'!

Conor

Thank you

Thank you God for giving me such wonderful grandparents, who love me and protect me, who help and care for me, and are always there for me. When I'm sad, they are kind, always nice to me and my sisters. My grandparents are the best.

Amen.

Alex Wynne

Take Care

Dear Jesus, thank you for my grandparents.
I love them and I always will. I will take
care of them just like they take care of me.
Thank you for minding them and keeping
them safe. Amen.

Rachel

Please God, will you keep my grandparents safe and sound; help them in every kind of way; and don't make problems for them like fires. Please keep them safe and tell me if they need anything. Amen.

Dylan Ralph

17

Long Life

Dear God, please take care of my grandmother, Margaret, and my grandad, John. Please give them health and happiness in life. Please, dear God, let them live for a number of years. Thank you, God.

Alice

Thank you God for Grandparents

Sometimes we take them for granted,
but look at what they do! They
always bring us sweets: lemon,
orange, strawberry and all
the other flavours too! They
are a shoulder to cry on when
you're feeling down. Without
them where would we be?
Grandparents are really special.
You really should know that. So thank
you God for grandparents.

Amen.   **Chris O'Donnell**

19

Bread and Honey!

Thank you God for my granny. She is very funny. She makes me bread and honey! Thank God she's very healthy. Gran will run or walk or skip. She's also very fair to us! Gran is a world-class baker with her bread and buns and tarts. And I know my granny has a big loveable heart! She makes us yummy bolognese and never has time to lay, for she's the best out of all the rest. Thank God I have my granny!

honey

My grandparents are **VERY SPECIAL**. They know what I love and enjoy. They give up their time and money so I can have a great time.

You always **TELL ME STORIES** and give me sweets. My parents are great because of you. **YOU RAISED THEM WELL**, it's true. I love you even though I can't see you. I don't see you often but **I LOVE YOU** anyway. Please God keep them safe, I pray!

Padraic Walsh

Dear Father,

bless my nannies in heaven
and my grandads in heaven.
Please look after them in all ways
because I love them very much.
Amen.

Saoirse

22

I love them

I pray every night

Dear Father, please take care of my grannies and grandads. They are in heaven. Will you tell them I love them because they were dead when I was a baby, except my granny Nora Ryan. But now she is dead. I pray for them every night. I draw pictures of them sometimes. Tell them that I am in second class and I am nearly eight. Tell them that Daniel (my new baby cousin) was born on the same day as Daniel Linhen's anniversary.

Amen.

Eimear

Thank you grandparents
for bringing my parents into
the world, because then in time they
brought me into the world. Thank
you grandparents for what you've
done, for my granny for making
me my favourite buns, and for
my grandfathers for hugging
me when their favourite teams
have won. Thank you God for my
grandparents. God bless them and
watch over them.
Amen.

Tanya Connolly

My grandparents
are very special
to me. I love them
like the blossoms
on the tree. They are
helpful for homework and
shelter and food. But the thing
I like about them the most is
their love.
Amen.

Shannon Kenna

25

Where would we be without our grandparents? They give us love and comfort. They are with us on special occasions. They make us happy and bring us for sleepovers. I love my grandparents. God bless my grandparents.

Amen.

Goodnight God, I'm going to bed, work is over, prayers are said. I'm not afraid of the night, but you will watch over me until morning light. Please, dear God, bless Granny, Pop, David, Uncle Pat, Auntie Mary, and all the other souls in Purgatory. Please keep them safe, happy and healthy. Thank you Lord for everything. Dedicated to Nora and Michael Jennings.

Amen.

D.E.

Look After Me

Thank you God for my grandparents because
they are really kind and they help me with my
homework and when I was young they bought
me sweets and brought me to football matches.
They looked after me when my
parents went away and
gave me good advice
and they helped
my younger sister
with a lot of
things. Thank
you God for my
grandparents.
Amen.

BLESS MY GRANDADS

Father in heaven, bless my grandads in
heaven. They are not with me any more.
I was a little baby and I never got to
see them. Please take care of them. I
pray for you and I miss them.

Amen.

Aisling Fennell

Dear God,

I would like you to look after Nanny and Grandad. They are kind, helpful, careful and generous and they look after Keelan and me very well. Will you make Grandad's foot better and will you make Nanny feel better? Amen.

Chloe

God, I thank you for blessing me with such good grandparents. They treat me nice, they give me money, they give me sweets and they teach me something new every time I see them. But God, I always wonder why you had to take them to heaven? Maybe you needed them to help you? Or maybe they were too good for us? Thank you God for blessing me with them. This is dedicated to my grandmother, Mary, and my grandfather, Brian.

C.M.

Nana and Grandad

Dear God, I love my nana and grandad for minding me most of the time. They also bring me on holidays in the summer to Ballyheige to their caravan. Sometimes my nana brings me shopping too. My grandad brings me to feed the ducks sometimes. I love them so much. Thank you so much for keeping them alive!

Lauren

I Pray

God, I pray for my two grandads and granny up in heaven and for my granny who is still alive. I pray that all of them are having a good time in heaven and on earth.

Amen.

We Pray

We pray for all our grandparents – we pray
for the ones who aren't alive and are
now in heaven; we love our grandparents
who are alive and remember those who
have died. We all hope that they will live
long, and then have a wonderful time in
heaven, and when we die we will go up to
heaven and meet them. We also thank our
grandparents for gifts they have given us.

Safe Home

I hope my grandparents are getting on well in England. I pray that they have a safe return on their flight from England to Knock and a safe journey home. I hope my other grandparents are well and healthy and my grandad's vertigo goes away. I hope they are all well and enjoying a healthy life.

Amen.

Peace Forever

Dear Lord, please bless and protect my two grannies. Keep them healthy and happy. Also please take care of my two grandads who died before I was born. Please give them peace forever. Help me to make them proud of me.

Amen.

Cherish New Life

Dear God, we pray for our grannies and grandads and hope that they have a nice life and let them enjoy the times they spend with family. God bless my grandad Mark who sadly passed away. Let him cherish his new life in God's hands.

Dear God,

we pray for our grannies and grandads. We hope they have a peaceful time up in heaven and on earth. We hope they live happy, healthy lives. Amen.

Aoife

This prayer is for my granny and grandad that have died. I hope you are safe up there. Bless them God. I love you and pray for you. Everyone misses you. We love you.

God Bless

My dear God, I thank you for my grandparents: Grandad, Nanny, Nanny G and my grandad who is with you. I love them and I know they love me. They all have had a nice few years, and I hope they have a nice few more. I am grateful that they can still stay home. They all live in little old houses and they are all very happy. Dear God, I thank you for my grandparents.

God, I pray

for both my grandads that are in heaven. I never met them but wish I did. I hope they are having a good time in heaven. From what I have been told both my grandads always tried to be optimistic and always had a good sense of humour. I hope they rest in peace.

Amen.

Good Health

To my grannies that are alive — I hope they have good health and live long; and to my grandad who is dead, I hope he has a good time in heaven.

May Granny and Grandad have good health, may their family be healthy and strong and a source of joy to them. Amen.

In My Sleep

God, please pray for my nanny
and grandad. Even though I
can't see them, I hear them
in my sleep. I love them more
than I can say.

Amen.

ear God, I wish and pray for my grannies and grandads. I hope that two of them are in heaven and are having a great time. And I also pray that my granny and grandad live to a very old age. Best wishes and love.

Dear God, keep my grandad and granny safe, keep them healthy and well, let them live for years more. Let my grandads be happy in heaven because I love my grandads and grannies. Amen.

Greatest Grandparents

I pray for my grandads Kirby and Scanlon, and I also pray for my grannies Kirby and Scanlon. They would have to be the greatest grandparents in the world. My grandad Scanlon would have to be the funniest grandad in Mayo. My two grandads are very strong and I hope they stay strong.

Amen.

A Good Life

I pray for my granny. I hope that life is good for her. I hope she has good health. Would you please help her when she needs help? And make sure she knows that I am grateful for all the times she's helped me in life. I love my granny very much, so please take care of her.

Amen.

We pray for all our grandparents who have died and are still alive. May they be blessed for their great work during their lives; and for those who are alive, may they enjoy many more years of good health. We ask God to protect them, for they are very special to us.

Amen.

Protect my Grandparents

Dear God, please protect my grandparents wherever they are and at all times. Please help my grandad's stiff ankles get better. Please let them live to a nice big age. If you grant me this I will be delighted. Amen.

Thank You Lord

Dear Lord, when my grandparents die,
please remember them and look after them
because I love them so much. Without them,
my life would be so different. They always
give and hardly ever ask for something in
return. Lord, please look after them always.
Amen.

Cian Fahy

God, thank you for giving me wonderful grandparents who are always there for me. They say prayers for me so I am saying one for them. God bless my grandparents. Amen.

Emily Ring

Dear Lord, I would love to tell you how much I love my grandparents and how much they love me. They care for me, love me, have faith in me; they will always be there for me. They make up the best bedtime stories and make up the best excuses. I love them so much. Amen.

A Shoulder to Cry on

Thank you loving God for my grandparents.
They are nice. They are with me night and
day, they help me on my way, with decisions
and faith. They are always there for me.
Sometimes a shoulder to cry on, sometimes
a storyteller, and even a source of income.
Please keep them safe.
Amen.

Oisin Lally

Wonderful Things

Thank you God for the wonderful things you have given me. Thank you God for my grandparents, great grandparents, and my granny who is still alive. For all the beautiful things they have taught us. When we go to visit them, all the sweets and chocolate they give us, so thank you for the things you give us. Amen.

Elisa Gill

Every night you cry or weep, your grandparents help you sleep. Every time you're feeling down, your grandparents help you cheer. Every time you get a boo-boo, your grandparents are there to kiss it better. Every time you're not in the mood for anything, your grandparents tell you stories of old days! And every time you hear this prayer, think of these times.
Amen.

Megan Crampton

DEAR LORD, thank you for the most wonderful grandparents — they are funny and can play with me. Some children have no grandparents. I am very lucky to have grandparents and they are very special to me.

Thank you God.

Liam

Dear God, thank you for my grandmother; although she may not be fine, it still warms my heart to know she is mine! Amen.

Cian Geraghty

Be Happy

Dear Lord, please keep my grandparents safe. They are kind, generous, loving, giving, and they're mine. Please, let them be healthy and happy.

Thank you.

Megan

kingdom of
Heaven

Dear Lord, have mercy on the hearts
of all my grandparents who have
passed away. Thank you for the time
I had with them. But now it is time
for them to leave the face of the
earth, and join you in your kingdom.

Kian F.

Wonderful

Dear Lord, thank you for my wonderful grandparents. Please keep my grandad alive for a good while, because Joe Joe is kind, loving, caring, and lots more. I wish they could live forever. I love them all so much. God bless my grandparents.

Ciara

lovely things

Dear God, my granny is very kind to me and I love her for who she is, not for what she does. She bakes me apple tarts and fairy cakes and lots more lovely things. She's the nicest person you could ever meet and we all love her very much. God bless her and all of us.

Rebecca Walsh

Dear Lord, I pray for my grandparents. I pray for them night and day. Keep them safe and keep them well. Some of my grandparents are not here right now, but they're always in my heart.

Daniel Flanagan

always...

Dear Lord, thank you for giving me the best grandparents anyone could have. Whenever I see them, they always smile, even when it's once in a while. They're always nice, they're always happy; they've been there since I was wearing a nappy!

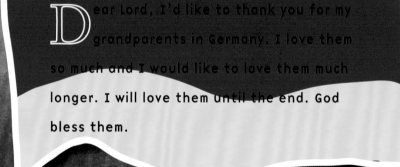

Dear Lord, I'd like to thank you for my grandparents in Germany. I love them so much and I would like to love them much longer. I will love them until the end. God bless them.

William Gill

Snuggles

Oh God, thank you for the wonderful gift of grandparents. Thank you for the surprises they give, the stories they tell, the problems they fix, and the snuggles they give.

Amen.

Sheena Campion

Gold to Red

Thank you God for my grandparents – the best in the world. I love them from gold to red; I love them because they're sweet and kind. They watch me play football. I love them so much. God bless them always.

Dearbhla

Dear Lord, thank you for my grandparents. They always help me when I need help and they always care for me. Lord, can you keep them healthy and always take care of them? I love my grandparents because they're always there for me when I need them.

Mark

Dear God, bless my grandparents for all the nice stuff they do for me. They give me money and bring me to the zoo. Thank you for my grandparents — they love me. God bless my grandparents.

I Love Them

Dear Lord, please let my grandparents live a little longer. Thank you for all you do for me and them. Sorry for asking for more. My grandparents do everything for me; they give me money even when I don't ask; they cook for me and I love them.

Matthew Brady

69

Dear God, thank you for my grandad. He was very nice to me and my brothers. He cheered us up with his happy smile. My grandad died in his sleep. We miss him very much. He'll always sleep in our hearts, through good or bad. God bless him and care for him. We will always love him.

Monica

family tree

Dear Lord, please mind my grandparents. They're very special to me — they're the people we look up to in our family tree. They may not be the fittest, they may not be able to jump, but they were the people who took care of me when I fell down with a bump. Dear Lord, please help my grandparents — they're special to me. They're the people I truly love in my family tree.

Bronwyn

Dear Lord, thank you for my granny. She is so kind to other people and to me. I like spending time with her. She tells me about her family's history. She tells me what happened years ago where she lives. And that's what I like about my granny. God bless her always.

Granny & Grandad

Thank you Granny and Grandad for taking care of me. The times you brought me places I wouldn't usually be, the times you helped me out with things, the times you prayed with me, the times you played with me. I love you Granny and Grandad for taking care of me. I love you Granny and Grandad forever.

Aimee

A Special Prayer

Dear Lord, I pray to you today to keep my grandparents safe in every way. Don't let danger come their way. Let them know I love them more and more every day and always let the sun shine on them. I pray for Grandad Mike in heaven that he will watch down on me. I end my prayer with a special 'I love you'.

Amen.

Lorraine

Safe...

My granny and grandad and my granny and grandad love me like my mum and dad. They protect me from danger and harm. When they are in heaven I hope they will look after me and watch over me.

Laura McCann

Dear God, thank you for my grandparents for all they do to make me happy. God bless my grandparents for the love and care they give me. God, thank you for my grandparents and bless them through their lives.
Amen.

God, as each day dawns, I think of them; God, as each day falls, I pray for them; and throughout my life, no matter where, in my heart they're always there. God bless my grandparents. Amen.

Dear God, my grandparents are kind and fun-loving and I would like if you could keep them healthy for years to come. They are kind and loving to me, and that's all I want. Amen.

Lift My Spirits

Dear God, thank you for my grandparents. They give me encouragement when I need it. They listen when I want to tell them something. When I am feeling down they lift my spirits and tell me that things aren't as bad as they seem. They are very special in my life. Please could you watch over them and keep them safe. Amen.

Take Care

Dear God, take care of my
grandparents in England. They
are always very good to me and
I love them very much. Also
look after my grandparents
in heaven as they look
over me. Thank
you for the gift
of such special
grandparents.

Aaron Bennett

For Keeps

Lord, we pray for all the nans and grandads. Keep them safe and happy and healthy. I thank you, Lord, for keeping my grandparents with me because they care for me and mind me. Thank you for making my grandparents special.

Dear God, thank you for giving me my grandparents. Please keep them safe and well. They mind us and care for us when we are sick and ill. We thank them for everything. Let them be around for more occasions and celebrations.

Amen.

We pray for our grandparents because they are very kind and generous. I ask the Lord to take care of my two grandfathers in heaven because they always took care of me. We thank the Lord for our grandparents that are still with us, for their encouragement and good example.

Amen.

The Spoils

My granny is good. She spoils me rotten. God bless my granny, God bless me, and God bless all my family. I love my granny.

Aoibheann Smith

On My Side

I love my grandparents. They bring me anywhere. Thank you God for grandparents. They are always kind and loving and they're always on your side and they never give out. Grandparents help you with your homework and even tell you stories about the past. I love my grandparents. God, please take care of my grandparents.

Amen.

Anne & Joachim

Oh God, thank you for our grandparents. We love them like Jesus loved Anne and Joachim. We love our grandparents because they listen to us and they're kind to us. They love us and if we do something wrong they forgive us. God bless them and take care of them.

Amen.

Close to Me

Dear God, please bless my grandparents.
All my grandparents love me. There's one
that hates bugs. I have two brothers but
they like me the best, because I always
leave them rest. Some may be gone to
heaven but they're close to me every
day. Please God keep them safe.
Amen.

My grandparents help me with things that are hard. I often help them to show I love them. They take care of me and they calm me down when I am scared. They tell me stories about God and how he loves us and it teaches me a lot about loving others. When I am sad they make me feel happy. May God be with them always.

Amen.

World's Best

My grandparents have been with me
all my life. They are the world's best.
They are happy and sad, they have
tried every test but nothing is better
than my grandparents. So please pray
for them and keep them here.

Ciara McKeon

Kindness

Oh my God, thank you for grandparents. They are the best. They give us lots of presents, but that's not all: they are kind and loving, and I wish they would live forever. Amen.

Robert

Dear God, I ask you to love and care for all of my living grandparents. When they pass away I would like you to still love and care for them and make sure they find happiness in heaven with you.

Amen.

Shannon Sheehy

Guide Them

God bless Nana and Grandad. On the road guide them, on a walk keep them safe, at work protect them, at home bless them. God bless my nana and grandad.

Thinking of Them

God, I pray for my grandparents.
As I rise in the morning I think
of them. While I am at school,
I think of them, and as I lie
down at night, I pray for their
health and mine.
Amen.

Heavenly Father up above, give my grandparents all your love. Guide and protect them every day, so that on earth they will enjoy a long stay. And when in heaven they are at rest, let them know they were the best. Amen.

Protecting

I know I never met you
but I know that you were
great. I know you're in
heaven looking over me. I
know you're protecting me
day and night. That's why
I love you, Grandparents.

I would like to thank God for my grandparents. All the times they comfort me. All the times they teach me new things. The smiles on their faces when they see me. How warm I feel when they hug me.
Amen.

God bless Granny, Grandad, Nanny and Pops – that's what nearly everyone prays at night. But the real wish is that they would stay forever, but we know that can't be right. So when you call our grandparents, tell them to bring slippers and all. Send a bubble to collect them, so they will have a peaceful journey up to heaven.

Aimée Carroll

95

Special

Dear God, my grandparents are really
special in every kind of way. I hope
they have good health and never pass
away. I pray for my grandparents,
Margeret and Micheal Danaher, who
are in heaven.

Amen.

Remember ...

Dear God, I love my grandparents.
My grandparents always want to see
me and I want to see them too. But
sometimes I am so busy that I forget
all about them. I still love them very
much. God bless my grandparents
because I love them and so do you.

Mairéad Nally

Let Us Pray

for my grandparents. Keep them
safe through illness or trouble.
We also remember the times
when they kept us safe when
we were sick. We thank them
for guiding us through life and
teaching us the faith of God.
Amen.

Wonderful

My grandparents are so wonderful.
They are also nice, neat and good.
My grandmother is still alive but my
grandfather is high above in the sky
watching me closely with you by his
side. Although you are not here with
me I can feel you beside me watching
what I do. So please, God, keep an
eye on my grandmother so she can live
on for years.
Amen.

W.T.

99

Thank you God for our grandparents. We love them so very much. They listen to us and chat to us; they bring us to Mass and go shopping with us. They make us happy when we're sad. Please take care of them when they are gone. Thank you for our grandparents.

Amen.

Rebecca Golden

Saint Anne

Good Saint Anne, in life my granny placed all her trust in you. Now that she and Grandad are gone to be with you, give them the joy of heaven. I ask that together with Joachim you will continue to look down upon my family and guide and protect us always.

Amen.

Thank you God for our grandparents and all the joy they bring to our family. Without you I cannot imagine life. Thank you Granny and Grandad for taking care of our parents, and for spoiling me.
Amen.

Joy

Little Angel

They'll always listen, they'll always care, they'll always be there, they won't care where. They'll always love me, they'll never forget. I'm always their angel, thank God.

My grandparents are funny, my grandparents are true, my grandparents always pull me through. When I am sad, all alone, my grandparents cheer me up with a song. So please God bless my grandparents.

Dear God, please keep my two grandparents safe no matter what, because they comfort me when I am sick, they mind me when I am scared, they warm me when I am cold. When I am scared they hold my hand and there is not a care in the world. They cared for my parents and they make me happy when I see them. They light up my day. Thank you.

Light Up

Dear God, this is just a message to say please pray for my grandparents every day; they deserve to be blessed for being helpful and kind and they light up my dark days in life, so pray for my grandparents on Grandparents' Day and bless them and keep them safe forever.

Amen.

There For Me

Dear God, please protect my grandparents every second of every day. When I was born they were there for me. On my first day of school they were there for me. My whole life, they cared for me. Please take care of them.

Amen.

Nicole

Say a Little Prayer

I think grandparents are great. They are helpful and kind. Sometimes they mind you and show you things you haven't seen before. Sometimes they show you how to kneel and pray in church. Grandparents are loving and cuddly. Sometimes they show you the places they played in when they were small like me. They comfort you when you are crying. They help you when you are sick. They give you stuff to play with when you are bored. When they tuck you in at night they help you say a little prayer that minds everyone.

Amen.

Sarah Burke

I want to pray for my grandparents,
but I don't know where to begin.
Do I start with how they gave me
money, so I didn't do without?
Do I start with how they stuck up
for me when my parents were giving
out? It isn't easy to put into words
how much I love them for,
not only do they give me sweets but
they also give me something that
means much more – their love.

Thank you God for my grandad and granny. They always help me. They always make me very happy, because they're my family. Thank you for my granny's lovely dinners. My grandad gives me lots of sweeties, even when I'm not allowed. I love my grannies and grandads very much. Now it's the end of the day so I must say goodnight and thanks for listening to me pray! Amen.

Jonathan

Long Life

Holy God, please pray for my granny and grandad who have had a long, healthy life (and are still alive). They had five children — four sons and one daughter, who is my mam. She is in heaven with you. They have loved my brothers and me for a long time. So pray for my granny and grandad to have a long life because I love them so much.

Amen.

Watching Over

Dear God, thank you so much for my grannies and grandads. They are not now among us but looking over me throughout my life. Please look after them while they are with you. They are not suffering now but happy. I hope they have a very happy life up there in heaven. I loved them even though I didn't see my granny and grandad McNulty. I will always treasure my memories of them in my heart. I will always love them throughout my life.

Amen.

I Love Best

Dear God, please bless my grandparents,
the grandparents that I love so much.
Please bless them at their breakfast,
bless them at their lunch, bless them at
dinner and bless them when they rest. Dear
God, please bless my grandparents, the
grandparents that I love best.
Amen.

Sweet Kind Caring

Dear God, I am asking you to bless my grandparents, who are loving, sweet, kind and caring. Please keep them safe in a loving home. They deserve to be blessed! I ask you to protect them always, through the people they meet.

Amen.

O my God, thank you for giving me lovely grandparents that I love. Please forgive them for when they make a mistake and thank you for making them so healthy. Please forgive me for when I argued with them or didn't listen to them. Thank you for everything about my grandparents.

Amen.

Grandparents
are Special

– I've got two. I love them both, so I pray
to you to keep them safe, all through the
night, and guide them through the day with
care. I love my other granny and grandad,
but they're deceased, so pray for them,
they'll rest in peace.

Amen.

My nana always wears lovely scarves and glasses. She loves chatting to me and babysitting me when Mammy and Daddy are out. I love my nana. God bless my nana. Granpa has a great moustache and he lets me rub it. Granpa always smiles at me and makes funny faces at me. My current obsession is dogs and Granpa has one. He has a little chat with the dog to let him know I am his friend. I love my granpa. God bless my granpa.

Granny, I thank you for everything you did for me, what you gave to me and when you cared for me. When I wanted you to be there for me you have been. I wish you and Grandad were alive because I'd be up in your house every minute. I miss your gentle nature, your caring ways and the way you were so generous to me. I miss the walks we had together, the way you showed me all of nature. You held my hand so tightly in case I might stray. You put your arms around me and showed me your loving way. May God put his arms around you now and take care of you like the way you cared for me. May the beautiful garden of heaven be full of the love you showed us while you were on earth. May God bless you and keep you safe forever until we meet again some day.

Amen.

Shannon Duffy

Dear Lord, thank you for my grandparents. They are very special to me. Please keep them safe and as healthy as can be. My grandparents are so kind and generous to me. They give me lots of money and sweets. If I didn't have any grandparents I don't know where I would be, so protect my grandparents and keep them close to me.

Sean McKenna

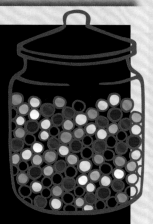

Being There

Dear Lord, watch over my grannies and grandads. Thank you for their kindness, for all the love they show in looking after me, for the way they're never too busy when I visit, for all the things they teach me, for the way they always listen to me, for making me feel special, for celebrating all my important occasions with me, for telling me about the old days. I want to specially remember my grandad that died; may he rest in peace in heaven.

Amen.

Colm Brady

Dear Lord, I thank my grandad for he always has a funny word to say. I thank my grannies for their wonderful baking and helpful advice. I thank the grandad that I never knew but I heard he was a great man. Amen.

Ernan Geraghty

119

Friendship & Advice

Dear God, thank you for my grandparents. I thank you for the friendship and advice they give to me. I thank them for the presents they give to me at Christmas, and on my birthday and at other times. I ask you to bless them for all their kindness and generosity to me. Amen.

Mary Tuffy

God Bless

Dear Grandad, may God bless you, may the gates of heaven be open to you. May you meet God and ask him questions you always wanted to ask him and may you make peace everywhere you go and may you help everyone ill and dying and may you be thankful for everyone thinking about you. Thank you for bringing me to and from Mass and school, thank you for being a great grandad. From your grandaughter.

Tara

Grandma's House

If I were in my grandparents' house they would give me a bed, food and drink. When I was younger they sometimes would look after me. God, I ask you to bless them, to take care of them and I would like to thank them for all the kind things they have done for me. Thank you God. Amen.

Catherine O'Toole

*L*ord God, bless all my
grandparents, for they always
care, they are there when I
need them, and even when I
don't. They always listen when
I talk, and always understand.
I will always love them; they
are very special to me.
Amen.

Katie Tighe

123

Lord, we ask you to bless our grandparents who are so special to us, and bless the time we spent together. May we listen carefully to what they have to say, and return the love they have always given us. May we always show our thanks for all they do. Please keep them healthy as they grow old, and may we always be able to help them as they have helped us. God bless them always.

Amen.

Katie Slate

Never Forget You

I will never forget you. God bless you because I won't have you forever, and I will love you always. Thank you God for my grandparents.

Cormac Hanley

Bless All Grandparents

Bless All Parents

Bless All Grandchildren

Saints Joachim & Anne Pray For Us
Our Lady Of Knock Pray For Us
Pray For Our Holy Father
Pope Benedict XVI

This Universal Prayer for Grandparents was composed
by his Holiness Pope Benedict XVI in 2008 for
The National Grandparents Pilgrimage

Prayer for Grandparents

Lord Jesus,
you were born of the Virgin Mary,
the daughter of Saints Joachim and Anne.
Look with love on grandparents the world over.
Protect them! They are a source of enrichment
for families, for the Church and for all of society.

Support them! As they grow older,
may they continue to be for their families
strong pillars of Gospel faith,
guardians of noble domestic ideals,
living treasuries of sound religious traditions.
Make them teachers of wisdom and courage,
that they may pass on to future generations the fruits
of their mature human and spiritual experience.
Lord Jesus,
help families and society to
value the presence and role of grandparents.
May they never be ignored or excluded,
but always encounter respect and love.
Help them to live serenely and to feel
welcomed in all the years of life which you
give them. Mary, Mother of all the living,
keep grandparents constantly in your care,
accompany them on their earthly pilgrimage,
and by your prayers, grant that all families
may one day be reunited in our heavenly homeland,
where you await all humanity
for the great embrace of life without end.
Amen!

Kate and her granny Kitty (Catherine)

The Catholic Grandparents Association was set up by Catherine Wiley, and for the past three years in September it has hosted the increasingly popular National Grandparents Pilgrimage in Knock, Co. Mayo. The mission of the CGA is to pass on the faith from grandparents to grandchildren. Catherine Wiley is a native of Castlebar, Co. Mayo, and now lives in Murrisk, Co. Mayo. She is married to Stewart, and is a grandmother of ten.

www.catholicgrandparentsassociation.com